Find Freddie Around the World

Find Freddie in the
United States
and...

- [ ] Alien
- [ ] Barbell
- [ ] Baseball player
- [ ] Beavers (2)
- [ ] Binoculars
- [ ] Carrot
- [ ] Cheese
- [ ] Cook
- [ ] Doctor
- [ ] Dog bone
- [ ] Dogs (2)
- [ ] Elephant
- [ ] Fire hydrant
- [ ] Football player
- [ ] Ice-cream cone
- [ ] Mice (3)
- [ ] Movie camera
- [ ] Octopus
- [ ] Palm trees (4)
- [ ] Rabbits (2)
- [ ] Skier
- [ ] Snake
- [ ] Snowman
- [ ] Stop sign
- [ ] Tent
- [ ] Trash can
- [ ] White House

Find Freddie in this Winter Wonderland and...

- ☐ Balloon
- ☐ Camera
- ☐ Caveman
- ☐ Deer
- ☐ Dogsled
- ☐ Dogs (3)
- ☐ Goose
- ☐ Harpoon
- ☐ Hockey player
- ☐ Ice skates (5)
- ☐ Indian
- ☐ Leprechaun
- ☐ Moose
- ☐ Periscope
- ☐ Police officer
- ☐ Rabbit
- ☐ Raccoon
- ☐ Refrigerator
- ☐ Sailboat
- ☐ Santa Claus
- ☐ Skiers (2)
- ☐ Spear
- ☐ Superhero
- ☐ Telescope
- ☐ Tent
- ☐ Tin man
- ☐ Tree stumps (4)

Find Freddie
in the
British
Isles
and...

- ☐ Artist
- ☐ Baby carriage
- ☐ Balloon
- ☐ Bicycle
- ☐ Big Ben
- ☐ Bow & arrow
- ☐ Clouds (2)
- ☐ Cow
- ☐ Double-decker bus
- ☐ Ducks (2)
- ☐ Four-leaf clovers (4)
- ☐ Fox
- ☐ Goalpost
- ☐ Golfer
- ☐ Hammock
- ☐ Horse
- ☐ Hot-air balloon
- ☐ Loaf of bread
- ☐ Miners (2)
- ☐ Mouse
- ☐ Mushroom
- ☐ Music notes (4)
- ☐ Pencil
- ☐ Rainbow
- ☐ Scarecrow
- ☐ Scooter

Find Freddie among these
Friendly
Foreigners
and...

- ☐ Anchor
- ☐ Antlers
- ☐ Baby
- ☐ Balloon
- ☐ Barn
- ☐ Bullfighter
- ☐ Camera
- ☐ Cheese
- ☐ Clothespins (4)
- ☐ Deer (2)
- ☐ Eagle scout
- ☐ Eiffel Tower
- ☐ Elephant
- ☐ Fisherman
- ☐ Greek ruins
- ☐ Kite
- ☐ Oil well
- ☐ Owl
- ☐ Panda
- ☐ Picnic basket
- ☐ Pigs (2)
- ☐ Pyramid
- ☐ Rain slicker
- ☐ Telescope
- ☐ Umbrellas (2)
- ☐ Viking
- ☐ Windmill

Find Freddie in this
Vast and
Exotic Land
and...

- ☐ Alligators (2)
- ☐ Bigfoot
- ☐ Black bear
- ☐ Bone
- ☐ Camels (2)
- ☐ Duck
- ☐ Elephant
- ☐ Gas pump
- ☐ Lion
- ☐ Magic carpet
- ☐ Mermaid
- ☐ Mongoose
- ☐ Monkey
- ☐ Mount Everest
- ☐ Mount Fuji
- ☐ Music notes (11)
- ☐ Penguin
- ☐ Rhinoceros
- ☐ Sailboats (2)
- ☐ Sheep (2)
- ☐ Snowmen (2)
- ☐ Soccer ball
- ☐ Star
- ☐ Suez Canal
- ☐ Tea bag
- ☐ Umbrella
- ☐ Whale

Find Freddie
in this
African
Adventure-Land
and...

- ☐ Alligator
- ☐ Ant
- ☐ Banana
- ☐ Bone
- ☐ Cat
- ☐ Crown
- ☐ Diamonds
- ☐ Donkey
- ☐ Egg
- ☐ Fishing nets (2)
- ☐ Fishing pole
- ☐ Flamingo
- ☐ Message in a bottle
- ☐ Moon
- ☐ Mug
- ☐ Mushroom
- ☐ Palm trees (3)
- ☐ Pyramid
- ☐ Rowboats (4)
- ☐ Santa Claus
- ☐ Seal
- ☐ Sunglasses (4)
- ☐ Surfboard
- ☐ Telescope
- ☐ Turtle
- ☐ Zebra

Find Freddie in the
Land Down Under
and...

- [ ] Apples (6)
- [ ] Barbecue
- [ ] Boot
- [ ] Cloud
- [ ] Cow
- [ ] Crocodile
- [ ] Doctor
- [ ] Eggs (4)
- [ ] Emu
- [ ] Fishing poles (2)
- [ ] Grill
- [ ] Guitar
- [ ] Lifeguard
- [ ] Message in a bottle
- [ ] Octopus
- [ ] Penguin
- [ ] Platypus
- [ ] Sailboats (2)
- [ ] Shark fins (5)
- [ ] Skiers (2)
- [ ] Snake
- [ ] Snowman
- [ ] Surfboards (9)
- [ ] Tasmanian devil
- [ ] Tennis racquets (4)
- [ ] Tire

Find Freddie in this **Blistery Blizzard** and...

- ☐ Airplane
- ☐ Aliens (2)
- ☐ Baseball
- ☐ Box
- ☐ Campfire
- ☐ Circus tents (2)
- ☐ Easel
- ☐ Football
- ☐ Heart
- ☐ Helicopter
- ☐ Ice castle
- ☐ Ice skates (6)
- ☐ Jack-o'-lantern
- ☐ Kangaroo
- ☐ Kite
- ☐ Magic carpet
- ☐ Paintbrush
- ☐ Periscope
- ☐ Santa Claus
- ☐ Skis (4)
- ☐ Sleds (5)
- ☐ Spaceship
- ☐ Stars (2)
- ☐ Tennis racquet
- ☐ Tin man
- ☐ Tombstone
- ☐ Top hats (2)

Find Freddie in South America and...

- ☐ Angel
- ☐ Ant
- ☐ Banana peel
- ☐ Bats (2)
- ☐ Beach ball
- ☐ Beehive
- ☐ Briefcase
- ☐ Candy bar
- ☐ Chinchilla
- ☐ Coconut
- ☐ Condor
- ☐ Dracula
- ☐ Flamingos (2)
- ☐ Iguana
- ☐ Jaguar
- ☐ Manatee
- ☐ Mouse
- ☐ Music notes (3)
- ☐ Ostrich
- ☐ Penguin
- ☐ Pig
- ☐ Shark fins (2)
- ☐ Skull
- ☐ Spider
- ☐ Tires (2)
- ☐ Top hat
- ☐ Toucans (2)

Find Freddie in Central America and...

- ☐ Banana tree
- ☐ Bats (2)
- ☐ Birdbath
- ☐ Bones (2)
- ☐ Broom
- ☐ Bucket
- ☐ Bull
- ☐ Cactus
- ☐ Camera
- ☐ Floating tires (2)
- ☐ Football
- ☐ Golfer
- ☐ Heart
- ☐ Hot-air balloon
- ☐ Kite
- ☐ Pie
- ☐ Piggy bank
- ☐ Pizza
- ☐ Police officer
- ☐ Princess
- ☐ Rabbits (2)
- ☐ Sailboats (4)
- ☐ Snakes (2)
- ☐ Tire
- ☐ Turtle
- ☐ Water skis
- ☐ Whale

Find Freddie on his Last Stop and...

- ☐ Apple
- ☐ Baseball player
- ☐ Beaver
- ☐ Cactus (2)
- ☐ Carrot
- ☐ Cow
- ☐ Cowboys (2)
- ☐ Dogs (3)
- ☐ Trash can
- ☐ Hose
- ☐ Mermaid
- ☐ Octopus
- ☐ Painted egg
- ☐ Paper airplane
- ☐ Parachute
- ☐ Periscope
- ☐ Refrigerator
- ☐ Sailboats (2)
- ☐ Sherlock Holmes
- ☐ Skunk
- ☐ Snowball
- ☐ Suit of armor
- ☐ Tents (2)
- ☐ Whales (2)
- ☐ Witch

Find Freddie and...

Apple	Dish	Hearts (2)	Pencil
Baseball bat	Fire hydrant	Ice-cream cone	Pizza box
Birdcage	Flower	Jump rope	Plate
Bucket	Football helmet	Mitten	Rocking chair
Candle	Frog	Moon	Turtle
Cupcake	Gift	Mouse	

LOOK FOR LISA: TIME TRAVELER

Look for Lisa in
Prehistoric Times
and...

- ☐ Baby carriage
- ☐ Candle
- ☐ Cherry
- ☐ Clothespin
- ☐ Dinosaur egg
- ☐ Faucet
- ☐ Four-leaf clover
- ☐ Hammer
- ☐ Hot chocolate
- ☐ Life preserver
- ☐ Message in a bottle
- ☐ Necklace
- ☐ Necktie
- ☐ "No U Turn"
- ☐ Palm trees (3)
- ☐ Periscope
- ☐ Piggy bank
- ☐ Pizza
- ☐ Skateboard
- ☐ Spool of thread
- ☐ Stars (2)
- ☐ Swimming duck
- ☐ Tire
- ☐ Volcanoes (2)
- ☐ Wooden wheel

Look for Lisa in the Creepy Castle and...

- ☐ Apples (2)
- ☐ Arrow
- ☐ Ball and chain
- ☐ Balloon
- ☐ Banana peel
- ☐ Baseball cap
- ☐ Birdcage
- ☐ Bones (6)
- ☐ Bowling pin
- ☐ Broom
- ☐ Calendar
- ☐ Carrot
- ☐ Crayon
- ☐ Door knocker
- ☐ Flower
- ☐ Flying bats (3)
- ☐ Football
- ☐ Ghost
- ☐ Jar
- ☐ Lantern
- ☐ Mice (5)
- ☐ Nail
- ☐ Oil can
- ☐ Paintbrush
- ☐ Pencil
- ☐ Rose
- ☐ Scissors
- ☐ Wristwatch

Look for Lisa at this Historic Happening and...

Look for **Lisa** as she **Rocks and Rolls** and...

Look for Lisa among these Exciting Experiments and...

- ☐ Apple cores (2)
- ☐ Arrow
- ☐ Axe
- ☐ Banana
- ☐ Bell
- ☐ Calendar
- ☐ Cannon
- ☐ Crayon
- ☐ Dart
- ☐ Doctor
- ☐ Fish
- ☐ Football
- ☐ Hamburger
- ☐ Hot-air balloon
- ☐ Jack-in-the-box
- ☐ Medals (2)
- ☐ Nut
- ☐ Piggy bank
- ☐ Puddle
- ☐ Sailboat
- ☐ Sardine can
- ☐ Scarf
- ☐ Shoelace
- ☐ Sock
- ☐ Spool of thread
- ☐ Spoon
- ☐ Totem pole
- ☐ Valentine

Look for Lisa in these
Cavernous Craters
and...

- ☐ Axe
- ☐ Banana
- ☐ Bucket
- ☐ Car
- ☐ Clown
- ☐ Coffee pot
- ☐ Cup
- ☐ Duck
- ☐ Earth
- ☐ Envelope
- ☐ Fish
- ☐ Flashlight
- ☐ Heart
- ☐ Key
- ☐ Kite
- ☐ Ladder
- ☐ Mouse
- ☐ Pig
- ☐ Pumpkin
- ☐ Ring
- ☐ Saw
- ☐ Shovel
- ☐ Stamp
- ☐ Stars (4)
- ☐ Stool
- ☐ Toothbrush
- ☐ Turtle

Look for Lisa in the Ocean and...

- [ ] Baby
- [ ] Barrel
- [ ] Baseball bat
- [ ] Basketball
- [ ] Boot
- [ ] Bucket
- [ ] Captain's hat
- [ ] Elephant
- [ ] Fish (3)
- [ ] Guitar
- [ ] Heart
- [ ] Homework
- [ ] Hot-air balloon
- [ ] Ice-cream cone
- [ ] Key
- [ ] Oars (5)
- [ ] Painting
- [ ] Palm tree
- [ ] Scuba diver
- [ ] Shark fins (2)
- [ ] Slice of watermelon
- [ ] Sock
- [ ] Surfer
- [ ] Tin can
- [ ] Tire
- [ ] Tree
- [ ] TV set

Look for Lisa at this
Special Celebration
and...

- [ ] Axe
- [ ] Barrel
- [ ] Basketball
- [ ] Bear
- [ ] Boat
- [ ] Book
- [ ] Bowling ball
- [ ] Chef
- [ ] Duck
- [ ] Ears of corn (2)
- [ ] Feather
- [ ] Fish
- [ ] Handkerchief
- [ ] Magnifying glass
- [ ] Mouse
- [ ] Owl
- [ ] Paintbrush
- [ ] Pizza delivery
- [ ] Pumpkins (3)
- [ ] Smoke signals
- [ ] Spoon
- [ ] Telephone
- [ ] Tepees (2)
- [ ] Turkeys (2)
- [ ] Turtle
- [ ] Watering can
- [ ] Worm

Look for Lisa at
Thomas Edison's Lab
and...

- ☐ Bandanas (5)
- ☐ Birdcage
- ☐ Briefcase
- ☐ Cat
- ☐ Chairs (2)
- ☐ Clipboards (2)
- ☐ Club
- ☐ Cookies
- ☐ Cowboy hats (4)
- ☐ Curtains
- ☐ Eyeglasses
- ☐ Film projector
- ☐ Fish
- ☐ Hammer
- ☐ Pail
- ☐ Periscope
- ☐ Picture
- ☐ Plant
- ☐ Rain slicker
- ☐ Roller skates
- ☐ Sailboat
- ☐ Screw
- ☐ Shadow
- ☐ Sheep
- ☐ Trash can
- ☐ Triangle
- ☐ Turtle

Look for Lisa among these Friendly Aliens and...

- [ ] Airplane
- [ ] Basketball hoop
- [ ] Briefcase
- [ ] Cactus
- [ ] Crayon
- [ ] Cup
- [ ] Desk lamp
- [ ] Donut
- [ ] Envelope
- [ ] Flower
- [ ] Hamburger
- [ ] Hose
- [ ] Music note
- [ ] "No Parking"
- [ ] Paintbrush
- [ ] Pencils (2)
- [ ] Pirates (2)
- [ ] Pyramid
- [ ] Straw
- [ ] Target
- [ ] Television
- [ ] Top hat
- [ ] Train
- [ ] Trash can
- [ ] Trees (3)
- [ ] Yo-yo

Look for Lisa at the Magic Show and...

- [ ] Apple
- [ ] Barbell
- [ ] Barrel
- [ ] Beard
- [ ] Box
- [ ] Burned-out lightbulbs (2)
- [ ] Dragon
- [ ] Elephants (2)
- [ ] Football
- [ ] Graduation cap
- [ ] Headband
- [ ] Heart
- [ ] Jack-o'-lantern
- [ ] Key
- [ ] Knight
- [ ] Leaf
- [ ] Mouse
- [ ] Puppy
- [ ] Purple hat
- [ ] Rabbit
- [ ] Sandbag
- [ ] Snake
- [ ] Top hat
- [ ] Weight lifter
- [ ] Trap doors (2)

Look for Lisa and...

Baseball bat	Cane	Moon	Sun
Bird	Fire hydrant	Octopus	Tire
Bottle	Fish	Rabbit	Top hat
Broom	Flowers (2)	Saw	Turtle
Cactus	Hammer	Scarves (2)	Wreath
Can	Kite	Snake	

SEARCH FOR SYLVESTER

Search for
Sylvester
at this
Mad Mall
and...

- ☐ Astronaut
- ☐ Balloon
- ☐ Barber pole
- ☐ Bone
- ☐ Bride
- ☐ Briefcase
- ☐ Cat
- ☐ Cowboy hat
- ☐ Feathers (2)
- ☐ King
- ☐ Ladder
- ☐ Manhole
- ☐ Moon
- ☐ Mouse
- ☐ Music note
- ☐ Parachute
- ☐ Pizza
- ☐ Robin Hood
- ☐ Sailboat
- ☐ Scarecrow
- ☐ Shopping bag
- ☐ Skier
- ☐ Stool
- ☐ Stuffed elephant
- ☐ Tin man
- ☐ Top hat
- ☐ Winter hats (2)

Search for Sylvester in this Fun-Filled Playground and...

- ☐ Arrows (3)
- ☐ Ballerina
- ☐ Banana peel
- ☐ Beach ball
- ☐ Birdcage
- ☐ Birdhouse
- ☐ Birds (4)
- ☐ Bone
- ☐ Bowling pin
- ☐ Cannon
- ☐ Diploma
- ☐ Dracula
- ☐ Ducklings (4)
- ☐ Eight ball
- ☐ Fire hydrant
- ☐ Flying bat
- ☐ Hockey stick
- ☐ Lamp
- ☐ Newspapers (2)
- ☐ Paint bucket
- ☐ Police officer
- ☐ Propeller hat
- ☐ Rooster
- ☐ Saws (2)
- ☐ Shovel
- ☐ Superhero
- ☐ Turtle

Search for
Sylvester
at
Fast Food
Heaven
and...

- ☐ Alligator
- ☐ Bat
- ☐ Bone
- ☐ Bowling ball
- ☐ Carrot
- ☐ Club
- ☐ Crowns (2)
- ☐ Dogs (2)
- ☐ Drum
- ☐ Elf
- ☐ Football player
- ☐ Frog
- ☐ Ice-cream cone
- ☐ Jack-o'-lantern
- ☐ Jogger
- ☐ Kite
- ☐ Mouse
- ☐ Owl
- ☐ Pickle
- ☐ Popped balloon
- ☐ Rabbit
- ☐ Shopping bag
- ☐ Skier
- ☐ Snowman
- ☐ Tire
- ☐ Trees (2)
- ☐ Tugboat

Search for Sylvester at the Zany Zoo and...

- ☐ Baseball bat
- ☐ Baseball caps (4)
- ☐ Bow tie
- ☐ Camel
- ☐ Fish
- ☐ Football
- ☐ Girl with pigtails
- ☐ Kangaroo
- ☐ Little Red Riding Hood
- ☐ Neckties (3)
- ☐ Owl
- ☐ Parrot
- ☐ Pig
- ☐ Pine tree
- ☐ Rabbit
- ☐ Raccoon
- ☐ Scarf
- ☐ School bus
- ☐ Sea horse
- ☐ Seal
- ☐ Shovel
- ☐ Spoon
- ☐ Telescope
- ☐ Top hat
- ☐ Toy turtle
- ☐ Trash can
- ☐ Turtle

Search for Sylvester in this Alphabetical School and...

- [ ] A
- [ ] B
- [ ] C
- [ ] D
- [ ] E
- [ ] F
- [ ] G
- [ ] H
- [ ] I
- [ ] J
- [ ] K
- [ ] L
- [ ] M
- [ ] N
- [ ] O
- [ ] P
- [ ] Q
- [ ] R
- [ ] S
- [ ] T
- [ ] U
- [ ] V
- [ ] W
- [ ] X
- [ ] Y
- [ ] Z

Search for Sylvester at the Basketball Game and...

- ☐ Alligator
- ☐ Balloons (2)
- ☐ Banana peel
- ☐ Baseball
- ☐ Bowling ball
- ☐ Cannon
- ☐ Cherry
- ☐ Envelopes (2)
- ☐ Eyeglasses (2)
- ☐ Football helmet
- ☐ Ghost
- ☐ Headbands (2)
- ☐ Hot dog
- ☐ Jack-o'-lantern
- ☐ Kangaroo
- ☐ Kite
- ☐ Lost glove
- ☐ Pail
- ☐ Pencil
- ☐ Pizza box
- ☐ Police officer
- ☐ Pom poms (4)
- ☐ Rabbit
- ☐ Snake
- ☐ Stars (3)
- ☐ Tarzan
- ☐ Turtle

Search for Sylvester at this Spooky Mansion and...

- ☐ Arrows (2)
- ☐ Bat
- ☐ Book
- ☐ Brush
- ☐ Bucket
- ☐ Candle
- ☐ Carrot
- ☐ Cauldron
- ☐ Curtains
- ☐ Flower
- ☐ Football
- ☐ Ghost
- ☐ Hammer
- ☐ Lawn mower
- ☐ Letter
- ☐ Old tire
- ☐ Piano keys
- ☐ Shovel
- ☐ Skulls (2)
- ☐ Spiderweb
- ☐ Sword
- ☐ Tin can
- ☐ Trash can lid
- ☐ Vulture
- ☐ Wagon
- ☐ Watering can
- ☐ Witch

Search for
Sylvester
at
Detective
Donald's Digs
and...

- [ ] Broken pencils (3)
- [ ] Calendar
- [ ] Can
- [ ] Candles (3)
- [ ] Chalk
- [ ] Chalkboard
- [ ] Cheese
- [ ] Comb
- [ ] Diploma
- [ ] Fan
- [ ] Fishing pole
- [ ] Hooks (3)
- [ ] Jacket
- [ ] Key
- [ ] Ladder
- [ ] Lamp
- [ ] Medal
- [ ] Nail
- [ ] Paint bucket
- [ ] Screwdriver
- [ ] Shovel
- [ ] Skull
- [ ] Snake
- [ ] Stack of envelopes
- [ ] Sword
- [ ] Tack
- [ ] Top hat

Search for Sylvester at this Silly Circus and...

- ☐ Balloon with star
- ☐ Barrel
- ☐ Cactus
- ☐ Cake
- ☐ Camel
- ☐ Cannon
- ☐ Clothespins (3)
- ☐ Clowns (4)
- ☐ Crayon
- ☐ Firefighter
- ☐ Flowerpot
- ☐ Lightbulb
- ☐ Mice (2)
- ☐ Necktie
- ☐ Party hat
- ☐ Pinocchio
- ☐ Pizza
- ☐ Police officer
- ☐ Skateboard
- ☐ Snowman
- ☐ Spoon
- ☐ Stars (5)
- ☐ Teacup
- ☐ Tin man
- ☐ Unicycle
- ☐ Witch
- ☐ Wizard hat
- ☐ Worm

Search for Sylvester as he Soars Through the Sky and...

- ☐ Banana
- ☐ Baseball bat
- ☐ Bathtub
- ☐ Bird
- ☐ Bow
- ☐ Carrot
- ☐ Cupcake
- ☐ Fishermen (2)
- ☐ Flowers (4)
- ☐ Flying bat
- ☐ Football player
- ☐ Guitar
- ☐ Moon
- ☐ Pot
- ☐ Scarecrow
- ☐ Scarf
- ☐ Shovel
- ☐ Spaceship
- ☐ Stars (3)
- ☐ Sunglasses
- ☐ Target
- ☐ Teapot
- ☐ Tent
- ☐ TV antenna
- ☐ Watering can
- ☐ Witch

Search for Sylvester in Bamboo Town and...

- ☐ Balloons (2)
- ☐ Brooms (2)
- ☐ Drum
- ☐ Eyeglasses (2)
- ☐ Fire hydrants (2)
- ☐ Football
- ☐ Football player
- ☐ Ghost
- ☐ Gift
- ☐ Hard hats (2)
- ☐ Heart
- ☐ Horseshoe
- ☐ Ice-cream cones (2)
- ☐ Jump rope
- ☐ Kangaroo
- ☐ Knight
- ☐ Mask
- ☐ Medal
- ☐ Octopus
- ☐ Pencil
- ☐ Periscope
- ☐ Record
- ☐ Socks (2)
- ☐ Stool
- ☐ Straw
- ☐ Telescope

Search for Sylvester and...

Apple	Carrot	Football	Paintbrush
Bamboo shoot	Cupcake	Horn	Screwdriver
Baseball	Drum	Kite	Spoon
Bone	Fire hydrant	Leaf	Top hat
Candle	Flag	Lock	Turtle
Cane	Flowers (10)	Moon	

WHERE'S WENDY?

Find Wendy at
Witchville
High School
and...

- ☐ Apple
- ☐ Axe
- ☐ Baseball bat
- ☐ Bear
- ☐ Bell
- ☐ Blimp
- ☐ Bowling ball
- ☐ Cauldrons (2)
- ☐ Dog
- ☐ Flying bats (2)
- ☐ Football
- ☐ Green hand
- ☐ Headless man
- ☐ Mask
- ☐ Mushrooms (3)
- ☐ One-eyed
  monsters (2)
- ☐ Pencil
- ☐ Piece of paper
- ☐ Scarecrow
- ☐ Shovel
- ☐ Skateboard
- ☐ Tire
- ☐ Tombstones (3)
- ☐ Turtle
- ☐ TV antenna
- ☐ Unicorn
- ☐ Walking tree

Find Wendy in the
Classroom
and...

- ☐ Baseball bat
- ☐ Bell
- ☐ Bones (2)
- ☐ Books (7)
- ☐ Broken egg
- ☐ Clock
- ☐ Eight ball
- ☐ Eyeglasses (2)
- ☐ Flying bats (2)
- ☐ Football
- ☐ Ice-cream cone
- ☐ Jack-o'-lantern
- ☐ Key
- ☐ Magic wand
- ☐ Needle
- ☐ Octopus
- ☐ Piece of chalk
- ☐ Pizza
- ☐ Rabbit
- ☐ Saw
- ☐ Skeleton
- ☐ Spiders (2)
- ☐ Stool
- ☐ Straw
- ☐ Umbrella

Find Wendy in the
Lunchroom
and...

- ☐ Apple
- ☐ Bird
- ☐ Broken nose
- ☐ Cactus
- ☐ Candle
- ☐ Cat
- ☐ Chick
- ☐ Cookbook
- ☐ Cymbals (2)
- ☐ Drum
- ☐ Flower
- ☐ Football
- ☐ Frying pans (3)
- ☐ Lighthouse
- ☐ Music notes (3)
- ☐ Paper airplane
- ☐ Plate of cookies
- ☐ Santa Claus
- ☐ Skull
- ☐ Snakes (2)
- ☐ Straw
- ☐ Teapot
- ☐ Trash can
- ☐ Turtle
- ☐ Volcano
- ☐ Yellow hand
- ☐ Yellow sock

Look for Wendy during Final Exams and...

- ☐ Ball of yarn
- ☐ Balloon
- ☐ Baseball cap
- ☐ Broken mirror
- ☐ Broken pot
- ☐ Brooms (2)
- ☐ Cheese
- ☐ Chicken
- ☐ Clipboards (4)
- ☐ Cloud
- ☐ Coonskin cap
- ☐ Doctor
- ☐ Duck
- ☐ Elephant
- ☐ Flying bats (3)
- ☐ Football
- ☐ Heart
- ☐ Jack-o'-lantern
- ☐ Lost mitten
- ☐ Magic lamp
- ☐ Mouse
- ☐ Pencil
- ☐ Saw
- ☐ Skulls (2)
- ☐ Stool
- ☐ Tombstone
- ☐ Trunk
- ☐ Worm

Hunt for Wendy at Graduation and...

- ☐ Barbell
- ☐ Bats (2)
- ☐ Bones (2)
- ☐ Broken mirror
- ☐ Brooms (3)
- ☐ Can
- ☐ Candle
- ☐ Cracked egg
- ☐ Dog
- ☐ Drum
- ☐ Ghost
- ☐ Graduation cap
- ☐ Guitar
- ☐ Hats with horns (2)
- ☐ Kite
- ☐ Marshmallow
- ☐ Moons (2)
- ☐ Music note
- ☐ Sled
- ☐ Target
- ☐ Tire
- ☐ Tombstones (13)
- ☐ Toolbox
- ☐ Umbrella
- ☐ Wizard

Find Wendy in
Count Dracula's Living Room
and...

- ☐ Airplane
- ☐ Baseball bat
- ☐ Birdcage
- ☐ Book
- ☐ Brooms (3)
- ☐ Chair
- ☐ Chicken
- ☐ Cracked egg
- ☐ Crayon
- ☐ Dustpan
- ☐ Mice (3)
- ☐ Mouse hole
- ☐ Mummy
- ☐ Owl
- ☐ Paintbrush
- ☐ Pig
- ☐ Pitcher
- ☐ Spiderweb
- ☐ Teacup
- ☐ Teapot
- ☐ Telephone
- ☐ Top hat
- ☐ Umbrellas (3)
- ☐ Vacuum
- ☐ Worm
- ☐ Wreath

Search for **Wendy** in Dr. Frankenstein's Laboratory and...

- ☐ Arrow
- ☐ Ball of yarn
- ☐ Banana
- ☐ Baseball cap
- ☐ Bat
- ☐ Bird
- ☐ Boot
- ☐ Bucket
- ☐ Candles (2)
- ☐ Cheese
- ☐ Clock
- ☐ Eight ball
- ☐ Eyeglasses
- ☐ Flowers (2)
- ☐ Fork
- ☐ Hammer
- ☐ Heart
- ☐ Lips
- ☐ Mask
- ☐ Mice (4)
- ☐ Needle & thread
- ☐ Pig
- ☐ Pizza
- ☐ Present
- ☐ Pumpkin
- ☐ Saw
- ☐ Spoon
- ☐ Stars (4)

Hunt for Wendy in the Mummy's Tomb and...

- ☐ "1st Prize" ribbon
- ☐ Bell
- ☐ Butterfly
- ☐ Cactus
- ☐ Cherry
- ☐ Cracked pot
- ☐ Fire hydrant
- ☐ Fish
- ☐ Giraffe
- ☐ Key
- ☐ Lobster
- ☐ Moon
- ☐ Mouse
- ☐ Painted egg
- ☐ Ring
- ☐ Rooster
- ☐ Sea horse
- ☐ Spiderweb
- ☐ Tepee
- ☐ Top hat
- ☐ Trunk
- ☐ Yellow bird
- ☐ Watering can
- ☐ Winter hat